Read for a Better World™

BEING SAFE ONLINE
A First Look

KATIE PETERS

GRL Consultant, Diane Craig, Certified Literacy Specialist

Lerner Publications ◆ Minneapolis

Educator Toolbox

Reading books is a great way for kids to express what they're interested in. Before reading this title, ask the reader these questions:

What do you think this book is about? Look at the cover for clues.

What do you already know about being safe online?

What do you want to learn about being safe online?

Let's Read Together

Encourage the reader to use the pictures to understand the text.

Point out when the reader successfully sounds out a word.

Praise the reader for recognizing sight words such as *my* and *you*.

TABLE OF CONTENTS

Being Safe Online 4

You Connect! 21
Social and Emotional Snapshot 22
Photo Glossary 23
Learn More 23
Index 24

Being Safe Online

There is a lot to do online! I play games. I watch videos.

I learn.
I talk to friends.

I stay safe online.

I don't give out my phone number.
I don't tell people where I live.

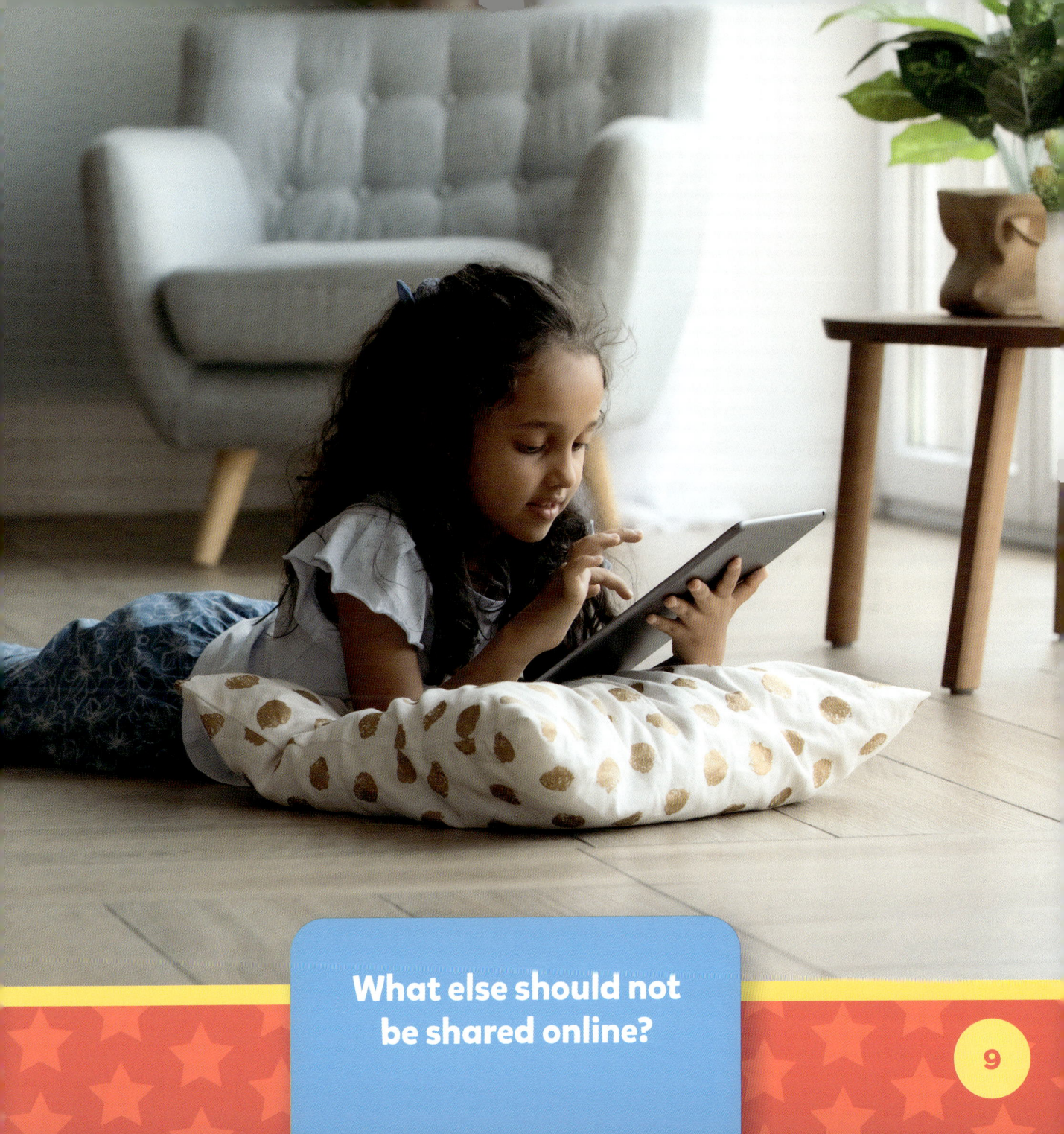

What else should not be shared online?

I ask my parents before
I put a picture online.

I ask them before I put a video online too.

Have you ever put a video online?

I don't tell anyone my passwords.

Do you play any games online?

I ask my parents before I get a new app or game.

I only talk to friends my parents know.

I tell a grown-up if someone is mean online.

I have fun and stay safe online!

You Connect!

What is something fun you do online?

What is something you learned online?

What do you do to be safe online?

Social and Emotional Snapshot

Student voice is crucial to building reader confidence. Ask the reader:

What is your favorite part of this book?

What is something you learned from this book?

Did this book remind you of anything you do online?

Photo Glossary

Learn More

Bassier, Emma. *Manners Online*. Minneapolis: Pop!, 2020.

Hubbard, Ben. *My Digital Safety and Security*. Minneapolis: Lerner Publications, 2019.

Morlock, Rachael. *I Am Alert Online*. New York: PowerKids Press, 2020.

Index

friends, 6, 16
games, 4, 14, 15
passwords, 12
phone number, 8
picture, 10
videos, 4, 11

Photo Acknowledgments

The images in this book are used with the permission of: © WavebreakMediaMicro/Adobe Stock, pp. 4–5, 23; © Backgroundy/Shutterstock Images, p. 6; © Rido/Adobe Stock, p. 7; © fizkes/Shutterstock Images, pp. 8–9; © Monkey Business Images/Shutterstock Images, p. 10; © FAMILY STOCK/Shutterstock Images, pp. 11, 23; © vectorfusionart/Shutterstock Images, pp. 12–13, 23; © DimaBerlin/Adobe Stock, pp. 14–15; © Kaspars Grinvalds/Adobe Stock, pp. 15, 23; © Sellwell/Shutterstock Images, pp. 16–17; © lev dolgachov/Adobe Stock, pp. 18–19; © Prostock-studio/Adobe Stock, p. 20.

Cover Photograph: © WavebreakmediaMicro/Adobe Stock

Design Elements: © Mighty Media, Inc.

Copyright © 2024 by Lerner Publishing Group, Inc.

All rights reserved. International copyright secured. No part of this book may be reproduced, stored in a retrieval system, or transmitted in any form or by any means—electronic, mechanical, photocopying, recording, or otherwise—without the prior written permission of Lerner Publishing Group, Inc., except for the inclusion of brief quotations in an acknowledged review.

Lerner Publications Company
An imprint of Lerner Publishing Group, Inc.
241 First Avenue North
Minneapolis, MN 55401 USA

For reading levels and more information, look up this title at www.lernerbooks.com.

Main body text set in Mikado a Medium.
Typeface provided by Hannes von Doehren.

Library of Congress Cataloging-in-Publication Data

Names: Peters, Katie author.
Title: Being safe online : a first look / Katie Peters.
Description: Minneapolis : Lerner Publications, [2024] | Series: Read for a better world. Read about citizenship | Includes bibliographical references and index. | Audience: Ages 5–8 | Audience: Grades K-1 | Summary: "It's important that kids know how to be safe online. With easy-to-read text and engaging photographs, this book makes digital citizenship simple for young children to learn"–Provided by publisher.
Identifiers: LCCN 2023011299 (print) | LCCN 2023011300 (ebook) | ISBN 9798765608722 (library binding) | ISBN 9798765624593 (paperback) | ISBN 9798765616468 (epub)
Subjects: LCSH: Internet and children—Juvenile literature. | Internet—Safety measures—Juvenile literature.
Classification: LCC HQ784.I58 P446 2024 (print) | LCC HQ784. I58 (ebook) | DDC 004.67/80289—dc23/eng/20230313

LC record available at https://lccn.loc.gov/2023011299
LC ebook record available at https://lccn.loc.gov/2023011300

Manufactured in the United States of America
1 – CG – 12/15/23